Cats

Children's Nature Library

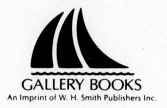

GALLERY BOOKS
An Imprint of W. H. Smith Publishers Inc.

8 7 6 5 4 3 2 1

ISBN 0-8317-6459-7

This edition published in 1991 by Gallery Books, an imprint of W.H. Smith Publishers, Inc., 112 Madison Avenue, New York, New York 10016.

Gallery Books are available for bulk purchase for sales and promotions and premium use. For details write or telephone the Manager of Special Sales, W.H. Smith Publishers, Inc., 112 Madison Avenue, New York, New York 10016; (212) 532-6600.

Written by Eileen Spinelli

Credits:
Animals/Animals: 48, 59; Henry Ausloos: 5, 10, 11, 12, 24, 47, 60; Norvia Behling: 6, 13, 41; G.I. Bernard/Oxford Scientific Films: 18, 24; Terry Cooke: 40; Marcia W. Griffen: 34; Michael Habicht: 14; Richard Kolar: 53; Jayne Langdon: 56; Zig Leszczynski: 38; Robert Maier: 31, 52; Joe McDonald: 27; Patti Murray: 23, 28; Oxford Scientific Films: 40; Robert Pearcy: 3, 4, 17, 22, 35, 38, 42, 43, 44, 51, 52, 56; Fritz Prenzel: 14, 37, 44, 57, 61; Michael & Barbara Reed: Front Cover, 1, 20, 63; Mike & Moppet Reed: 10, 45, 64; Ralph A. Reinhold: 30; LLT Rhodes: 28; Leonard Lee Rue, III: 50; Donald Specker: 32, 42; Stouffer Enterprises, Inc.: 30; Al Thomas: 8; Sydney Thomson: 6, 8, 9, 12, 16, 18, 20, 26, 29, 33, 36, 48; **Gail Denham:** 39; **Gerry Ellis Wildlife:** Gerry Ellis: Back Cover, 49, 62; **Dorothy Holby:** 4, 7, 12, 15, 19, 21, 22, 25, 34, 36, 46, 54, 55, 58, 62.

Table of Contents

History of Cats

Cats were first kept by the ancient Egyptians, who considered them part of the family. They were respected and were often presented with gifts of precious jewels. When a cat died, it was given an elaborate funeral. To express their grief at the death of a house cat, family members shaved their eyebrows. Killing a cat was a very serious crime. Eventually, this respect for cats turned to worship. Cats came to be considered gods.

History of Cats

People believe that the Egyptians taught cats how to catch mice and rats. When word of this "rodent hunter" spread, Europeans became quite interested, since they were plagued by mice and rats. Unfortunately, Egyptian law did not allow cats to be taken from the country. Somehow, foreign traders smuggled these Egyptian cats onto ships bound for Europe. Prized at first for their fine mousing skills, cats were later valued for their companionship as well.

Cat Tales & Superstitions

- The ancient Romans thought black cats were lucky. Today many people think they are unlucky.

- In seaports of long ago, a fisherman's wife kept a cat in her home until her husband returned. If the cat ran away, it was considered a sign that the boat was in trouble.

- Another old tale: A cat found sitting by the front door before a wedding is a sure sign of bad things to come.

Cats' Coats & Colors

A cat's coat is soft and silky. Cats come in many colors, including black, white, and gray. There are orange cats and tawny golden cats. Cats can also be spotted, patched, or striped.

Some cats have long, thick hair. Other cats have short hair. Rex cats have wavy hair. Most cats are smooth to touch. The coats of newborn kittens often feel like fuzzy duckling down.

Cats' Whiskers

A cat's whiskers aren't there just to look cute.
They have important work to do. Whiskers guide
a cat through tall grass. They help a cat prowl a
path through the darkness. They
also tell a cat if a space is big
enough to pass through. When
a cat is angry, its whiskers
bristle. When a cat is sick,
its whiskers droop down.

12

Cats' Eyes

A cat's eyes shine at night. Ancient Egyptians believed the glow in a cat's eyes at night was the sun. They believed cats could see in total darkness. Egyptians named the cat *Mau* (mow), which means "to see."

Cats cannot see in total darkness. But they can see much better in the dark than we can. They also prefer shade and darkness to bright light. Cats cannot see colors—they are color-blind.

Cats in Action

Cats run, jump, chase, and pounce. They like nosing around trees, shelves, and stone walls. A cat's tail helps it keep its balance—cats almost always have a gentle landing when they fall.

Did you ever wonder why your cat rubs against your leg? It is your cat's way of marking its scent and to say, "This is my person." Rubbing can also be a sign of affection.

Cats also scratch, but they don't scratch just because they like to. They *need* to scratch. Scratching keeps a cat's claws trim and its muscles fit. Outdoor cats scratch on tree trunks and fences. Indoor cats need a special scratching post. Unless, of course, you don't mind the stuffing getting scratched out of your sofa!

Cats in Action

If a cat doesn't get much chance to run and chase, it builds up energy. This energy may erupt into a mad dash all through the house. Indoor cats do this more often than outdoor cats.

Have you ever noticed the cat activity called kneading? A cat kneads with its paws as though it were making bread. This quaint action means, "I am happy."

Cat Play

Give a cat a piece of crumpled paper and it will play ball. Give it a big paper bag, and it will frolic inside of it. It can bat an old sock around the room for hours. Cats will also happily pounce on dustballs, bits of sunlight, and your big bare toe. Even lazy cats can be coaxed into playing. Try surprising an idle cat with a perky catnip toy.

Cats & Water

Cats can swim, but remember: Cats hate water. But they do love to watch water. A cat will stare at a dripping faucet for hours. It might even try to catch the drops on its tongue.

There is one type of cat that likes water. The Turkish Van cat loves both watching and wading. It is always eager to splash and swim.

Cats & Grooming

The first lesson mother cat teaches her kittens is grooming. At first, mother washes and grooms her kittens. Then, the kittens learn how to wash and groom themselves. Finally, they have fun washing and grooming one another. Grooming keeps cats clean. It also keeps them cool on hot days. A cat has its own built-in washcloth—its tongue.

24

Cats' Eating Habits

When it comes to eating, cats are finicky. They don't like cold food or deep dishes. If you try to feed your cat from a dirty dish, it might turn up its nose and walk away. Cats also don't like eating under bright lights or where there is a lot of noise. They don't like sweets, either. What they do like is eating at the same time each day.

Cats as Hunters

Cats chase lots of creatures—insects, birds, and even fish. They may even pounce on fur-trimmed coats. But cats are most famous as hunters of mice and rats. Usually, a cat will not eat its prey at the scene of the catch. Instead, it takes it to a more private place. When a cat wants to show off, it will present its catch as a gift to its owner.

Cat Chat

Cats are chatty creatures. Not only do they "talk" with their voices, they also talk with their tails, fur, backs, and paws. A cat that is teased or annoyed may arch its back and raise its fur. Cat paws rattle doorknobs and scratch at windows to say, "Let me in!" When a cat purrs, it may be saying, "I'm contented."

An angry cat will spit and hiss. A jealous cat will growl. The tiny meow at the door says, "Thank you for letting me in." A clicking noise boasts, "I see a mouse." Tails talk like this: Soft waving means, "Gee, I'm pleased"; beating or wagging announces, "I'm upset"; and a fluffy tail pleads, "Help, I'm scared."

Cat Naps

Cats like soft, snug sleeping places. They like to nap high up—like on top of your refrigerator. Other cats choose a favorite armchair, so look before you sit!

Kittens enjoy a cozy, cardboard box, especially if there is a nice, hot-water bottle inside. Cats also enjoy window ledges for daytime naps. At night, most cats prefer sleeping in the best place in the house—your bed.

Mother Cats

After her kittens are born, mother cat stays close by. If anyone comes near her kittens, she will scold them loudly. She may even move her

babies to a new and safer place if she feels they are in danger. Mother cat spends most of her time feeding and grooming her kittens. Often, she will join in their play. Mother cat knows her kittens have important lessons to learn. She is a skilled and patient teacher.

Kittens

Newborn kittens want to do nothing but sleep and eat. If they happen to tumble out of the nest, they will cry until their mother fetches them. As they get bigger, they become curious and playful.

They snoop in cupboards, peek around doorways, and chase after toys, leaves, and the taunting tails of their littermates. They nibble on, pounce on, and play-fight with other kittens.

Indoor Cats

Indoor cats choose a favorite spot to call their own—like a comfy chair or a corner of a rug. Can't find your indoor cat? It may be playing hide-and-seek! Check under the bed or in your sock drawer.

Indoor cats must have scratching posts to keep their claws sharp. If you want to pamper your indoor cat, set out a pot of grass for nibbling.

Outdoor Cats

Your outdoor cat should not get lost. It has fine-tuned homing instincts. Outdoor cats mark their territory. Neighbor cats can "read" this marking, much the way we might read a "Private Property" sign. Outdoor cats often make friends with other cats in the neighborhood. They have fun climbing trees, chasing milkweed puffs, and relaxing in the shade. Please don't shut your cat out all night—it might get hurt.

Shorthaired Cats

Shorthaired cats come to us from Egypt, Europe, and the Far East. Their short hair makes them easy to care for—they need combing and brushing only once a week. These cats shed a little hair at a time throughout the year. Shorthairs love batting at ping-pong balls and crumpled newspapers. They tend to be noisier than their long-haired cousins.

Long-haired Cats

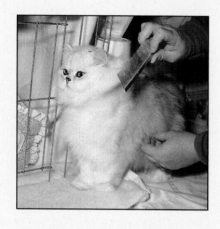

Long-haired cats need to be combed and brushed every day. In spring and fall, they shed a lot of their hair. Many long-haired cats like to snuggle into cozy places such as baskets, rolled-up rugs, and small paper boxes. Their voices are softer than the voices of shorthairs. These cats are usually stay-at-homes.

Unusual Cats

Did you know that there is a cat with no tail? This cat is called the Manx (manks). One legend says that the Manx cat lost its tail coming aboard Noah's ark. How? It got caught in the door.

The Sphynx cat has a tail—it's the fur that's missing. Its skin is warm and smooth. The Sphynx cat is the perfect pet for folks who don't like vacuuming.

Alley Cats

Many cats have good homes. The alley cat has no home at all. It wanders around the streets, toppling trash cans looking for food. In the rain, it huddles in doorways. The alley cat is often cold, nervous, and scared. Most of these sad strays are picked up by animal shelters. Some are lucky enough to be adopted by caring families.

Cat Trivia

Did you know?

- A group of cats is called a clowder.
- Many white cats are born deaf.
- Cats don't like to be stared at.
- June is Adopt-a-Cat Month.
- Healthy cats have cool, wet noses.
- Cats run faster than dogs of the same size.
- Whistling irritates many cats.

Siamese

Siamese (SY-uh-MEEZ) cats are bright and easy to train. They are good travelers— they enjoy a Sunday drive in the car. Siamese cats also like plenty of attention. They are very elegant-looking with their sapphire-blue eyes. You might expect a Siamese cat to have a dainty voice, but it doesn't. Its voice is noisy and shrill.

Abyssinian

The Abyssinian (AB-uh-SIN-ee-uhn) cat has
several names. It has been called "the rabbit cat,"
"the desert cat," and "the little lion." Today,
most cat-lovers refer to the Abyssinian fondly as
"Aby." The Abyssinian cat needs plenty of
space—it loves to run and climb trees. This cat
has pretty, almond-shaped eyes that are
sometimes golden and sometimes green. The
Abyssinian cat also has a soft, bell-like voice.

Himalayan

The Himalayan (HIM-uh-LAY-uhn) cat is a cross between a Persian and a Siamese. "Himmies," as they are affectionately known, are friendly and quite "talkative." These cats become especially attached to their owners.

This cat's color patterns are also seen in certain mice and rabbits. It even got its name from the Himalayan rabbit. Himmies have large heads, snub noses, and deep blue eyes.

Birman

Birman (BUR-muhn) cats once lived in the temples of Burma where they were treated as sacred cats. Often, they were given away as precious gifts to rulers in the Orient.

The Birman cat has white "gloves" on all four paws. Of course, these are not real gloves, but the cat's own hair. The Birman's long, silky coat needs daily grooming. It is friendly and intelligent.

Russian Blue

The Russian Blue cat used to be called the Archangel cat. It came to England with some Russian sailors from the seaport of Archangel. Russian rulers prized this cat very much.

The Russian Blue is a quiet cat. It seldom uses its voice. When it does, the sounds it makes are soft and silvery. It is a gentle and shy cat.

American Shorthair

Some people believe that the American shorthair was brought to America on the *Mayflower* by the Pilgrims. This may be true, since cats were often brought aboard ships to kill rats and mice. Later, these cats crossed America in covered wagons with the early pioneers.

The American shorthair is hardy and rugged. It enjoys the outdoors. It is also affectionate and gentle with children.